Introducing The Positions...

for VIOLA—Vol. I THIRD and HALF POSITIONS

There are many students today, who, after an elementary training on the viola, restricted entirely to the *first* position of their instrument, find themselves unable to participate in the activities of amateur orchestras and ensembles, due to their inability to play in the higher positions of their instrument. Neither can they perform much in the way of available solo literature, due to their limited technic. From a practical standpoint, there are five higher positions on the viola, in addition to a so-called *half* position, which is sometimes referred to as the "saddle" or "nut" position.

INTRODUCING THE POSITIONS for Viola, Volume One, takes up the study of the *third* position, followed by the *half* position. The *third* position should at all times be given first consideration, for not only is it the easiest to play of all the higher positions (due to the convenience afforded in resting the left hand against the edge of the instrument), but also it is used more in actual performance than any of the other higher positions. By going directly from the *first* to the *third* position, students learn to play positions in the exact manner in which they will use them most frequently. Furthermore, when following the procedure of taking up the *third* position before the *second* position, students are given an early opportunity to begin the very important study of shifting, which unfortunately, is neglected in nearly all viola methods dealing with position study in the traditional manner. Following the study of the *third* position, the next position to be taken up in relative importance, is the *half* position. Students who follow the system of alternate fingerings offered by this position are able to simplify many complicated passages and avoid awkward stretches of the fingers, especially when playing in sharp keys.

INTRODUCING THE POSITIONS for Viola, Volume Two, is a continuation of the course of study presented in Volume One, and includes the study of the *second, fourth* and *fifth* positions, as well as the introduction of the treble clef, which is used frequently in viola music to avoid the use of innumerable ledger lines when extremely high notes are employed.

INTRODUCING THE POSITIONS for Viola, Volumes One and Two, constitute together, an introductory course of position playing for the viola. For additional material of a more advanced nature, the famous viola school by Ritter, and the equally famous method of Cavallini, are recommended, as well as the many excellent etudes of Hoffmeister, Bruni, Blumenstengel, Palaschko, Schoen, Campagnoli, Kreutzer, Fiorillo, Rode, and others. In addition, the orchestral works of Wagner, Richard Strauss, Berlioz, and similar operatic and symphonic composers may be used. From these sources a wealth of advanced material utilizing higher positions on the viola is available.

Harvey S. Whistler, Ph. D.

HAL•LEONARD CORPORATION
7777 W. BLUEMOUND RD. P.O. BOX 13819 MILWAUKEE, WI 53213

In memory of Emil Ferir, whose viola playing and musical ideals were an inspiration to the author in preparing the present work.

The Third Position

Preparatory Studies in the Key of F Major

⌐——¬ = Half-step; fingers close together

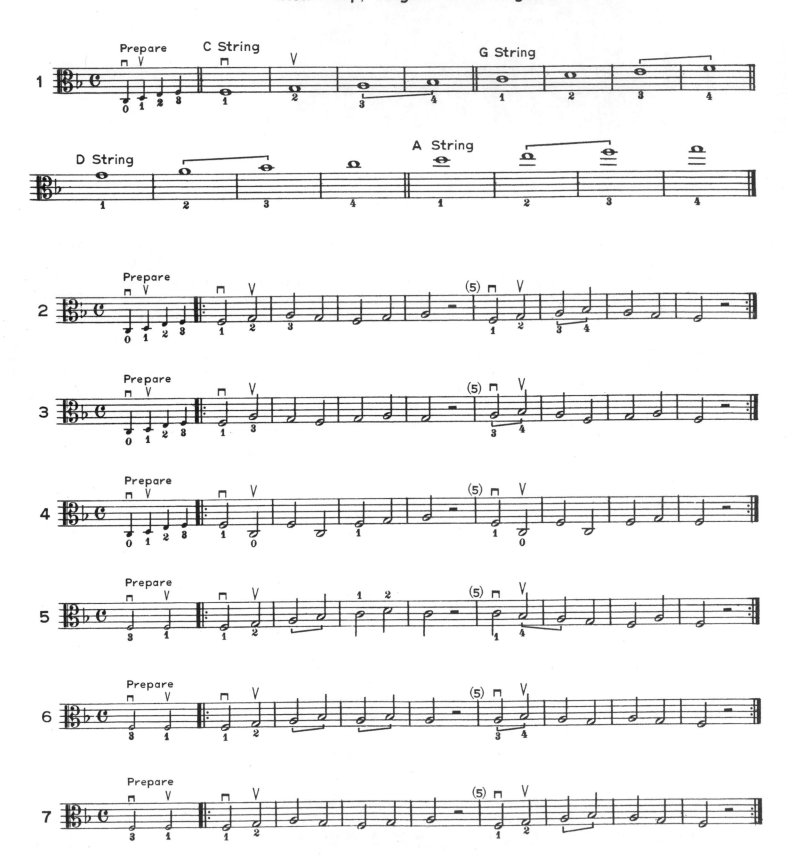

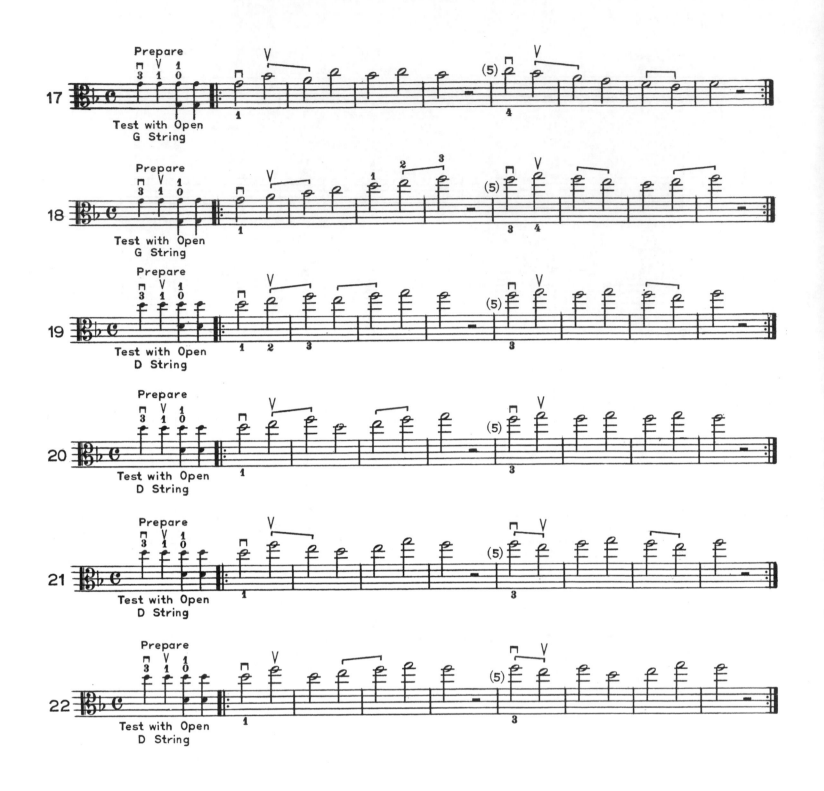

Scale Study

Third Position Etude

CAMPAGNOLI

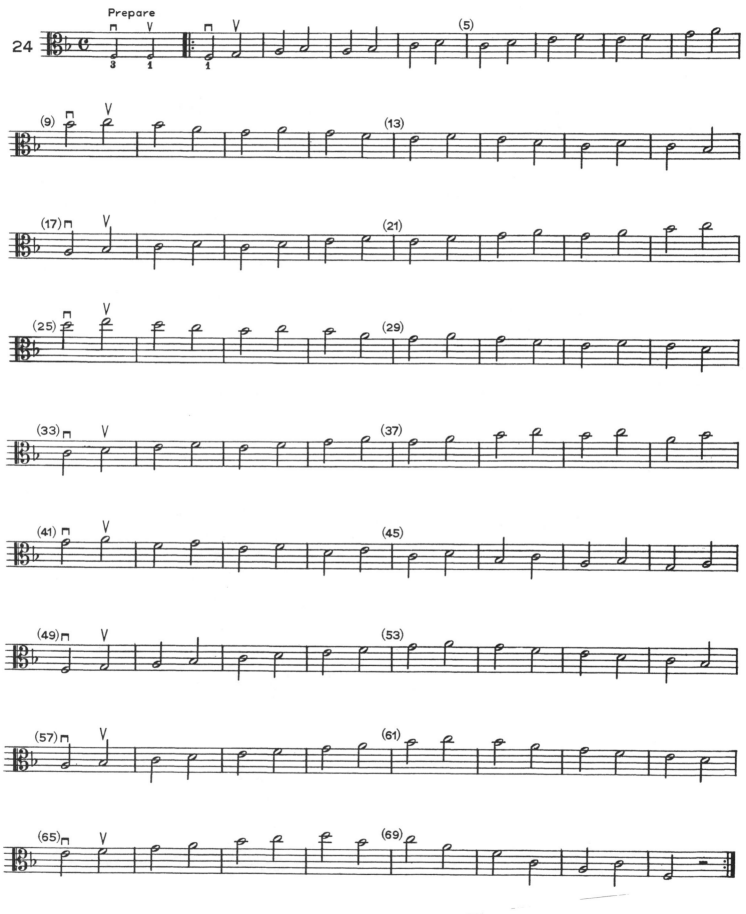

Selected Studies in the Third Position

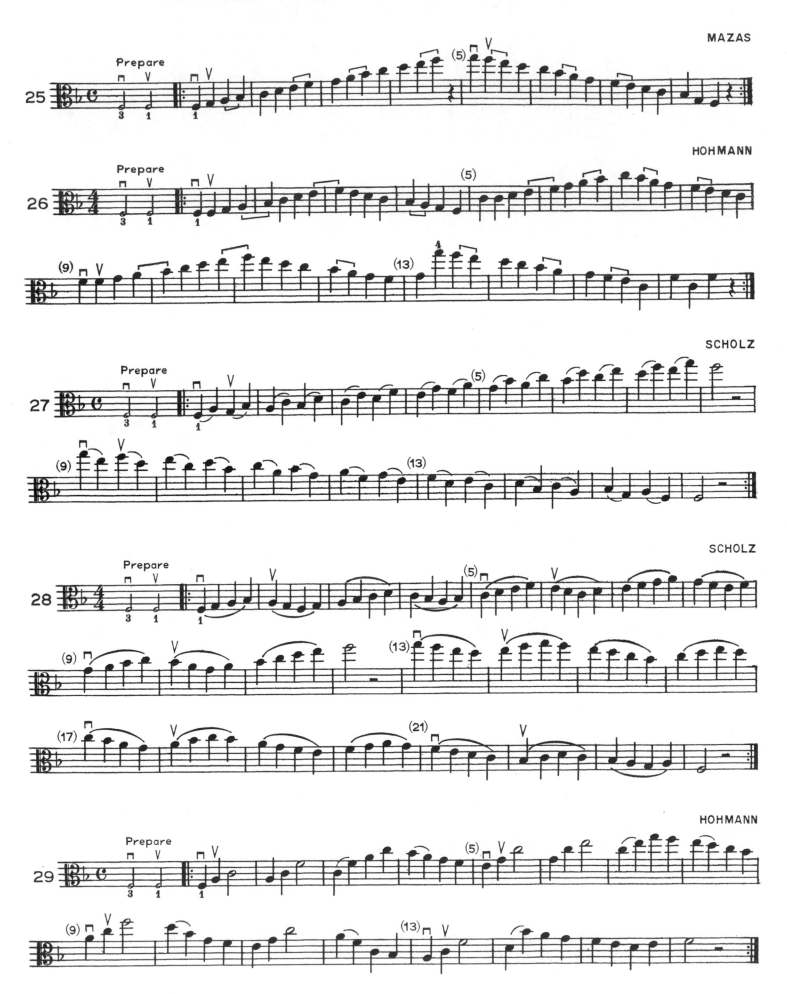

Shifting from First to Third Position

When shifting from the first to a higher position, do not take the finger up and put it down again, instead, *slide* into the higher position.

A String

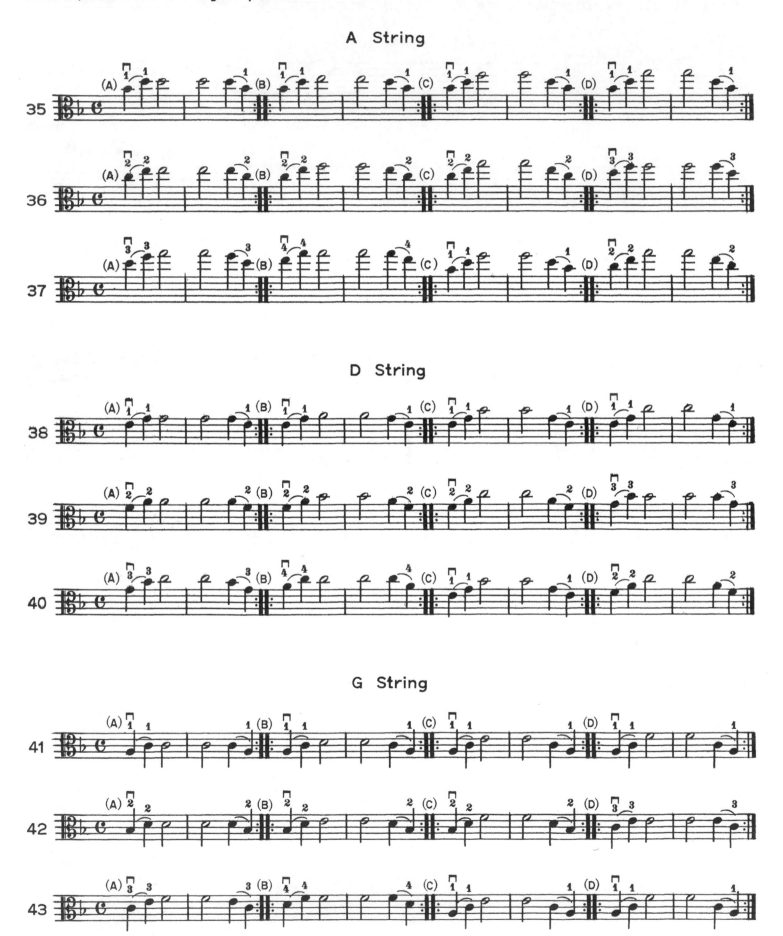

D String

G String

C String

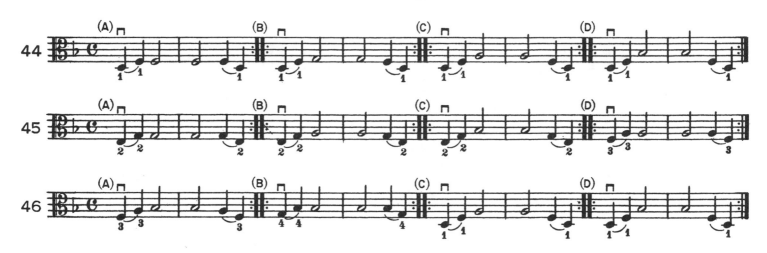

Shifting from One Finger to Another

The student should shift forward on the finger that was last down, and likewise, shift backward on the finger that was last down.

The small notes in the exercises below indicate the movement of the fingers in shifting, and as the student perfects his ability to shift from one note to another, the small notes eventually should not be heard.

Key of C Major

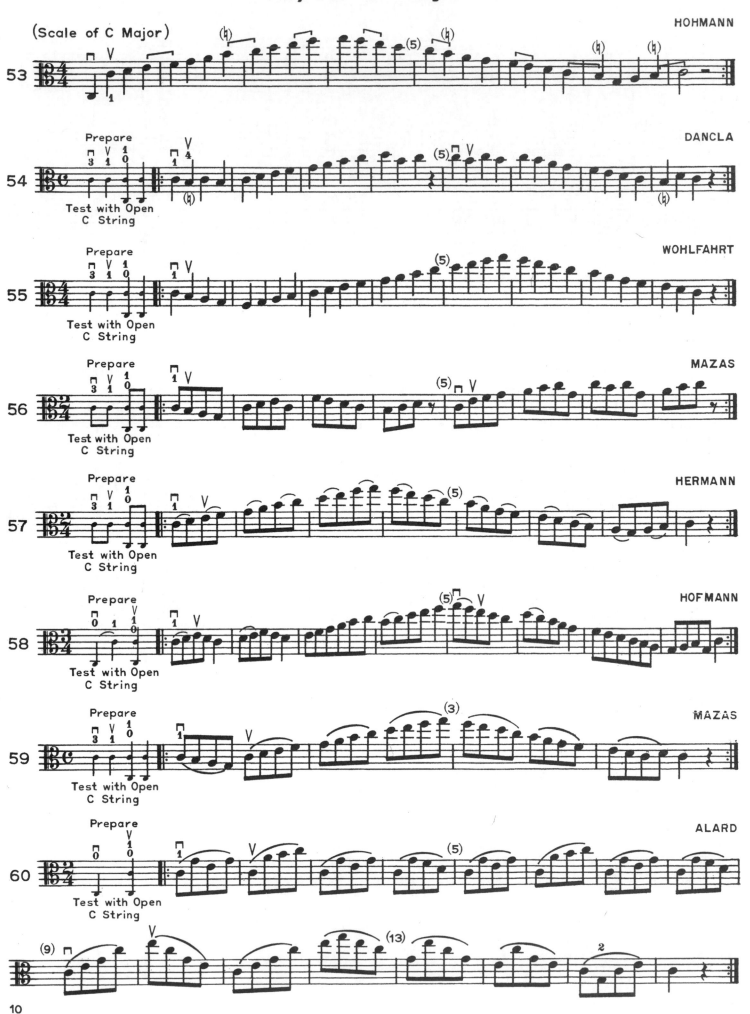

Shifting in Key of C Major

Shifting from One Finger to Another

Key of G Major

Shifting

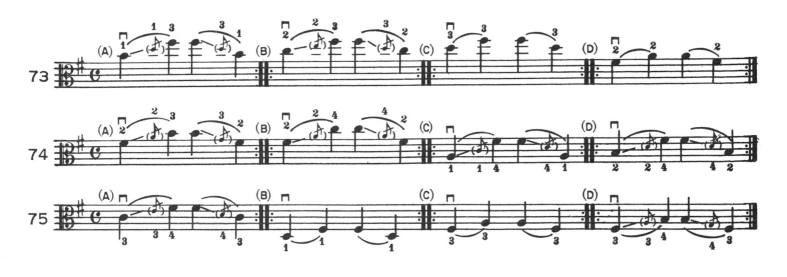

Advanced Shifting Exercises

SCHOLZ

Combining First and Third Positions

Ip. = First Position   IIIp. = Third Position

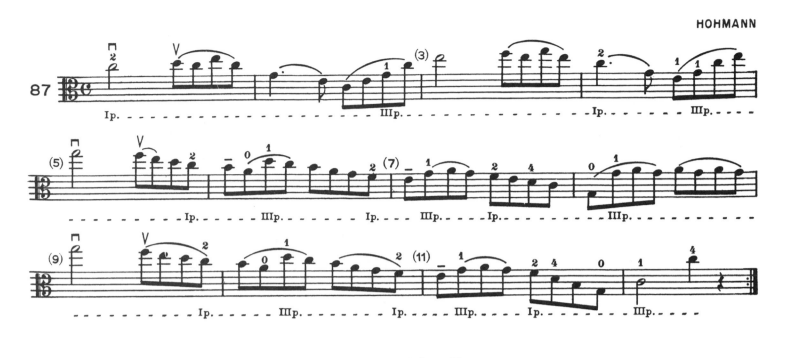

HOHMANN

Shifting Studies

SCHOLZ

Shifting Study

DANCLA

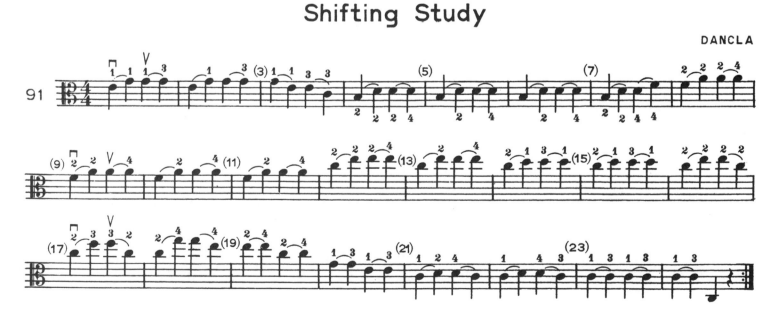

Key of Bb Major

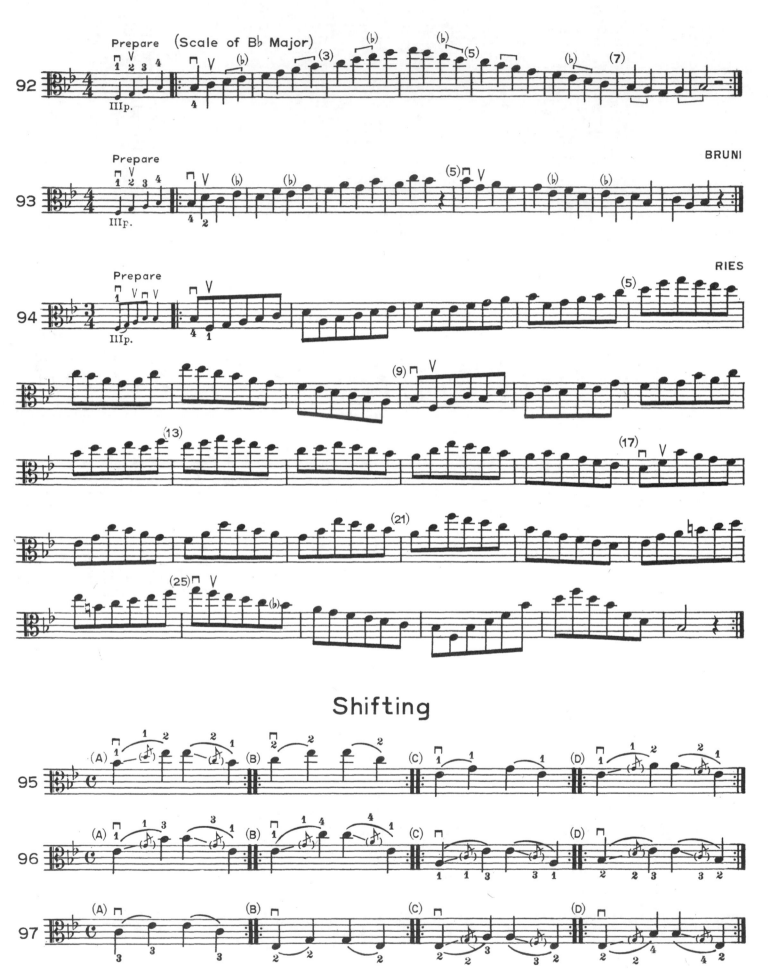

Shifting

Key of E♭ Major

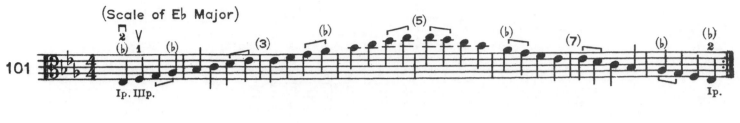

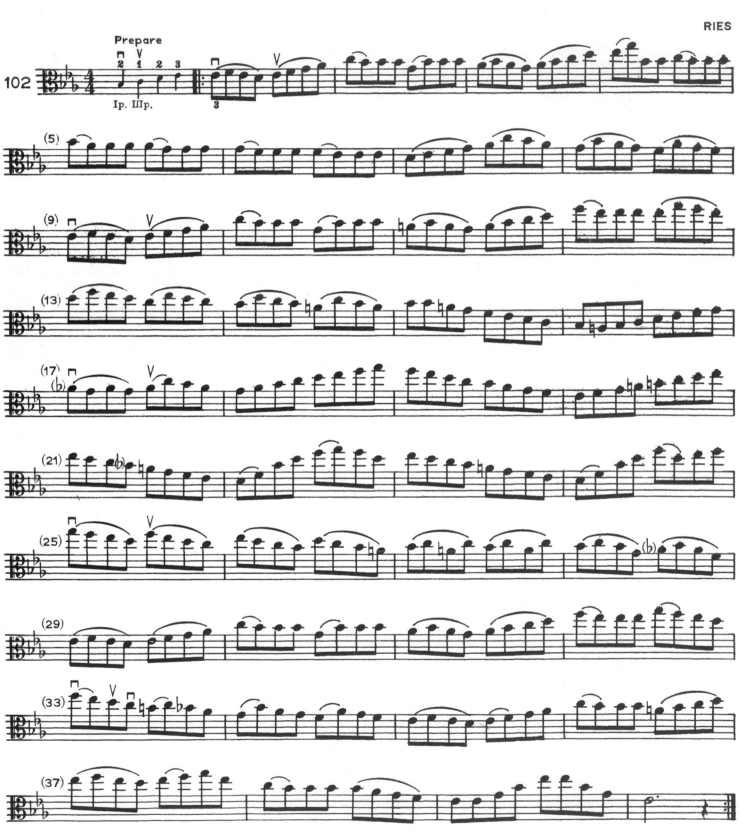

Shifting

Key of D Major

Shifting

20

SCHOLZ

WOHLFAHRT

Natural Harmonics

To produce a natural harmonic, extend the fourth finger forward, and merely touch it lightly against the string; *do not* press the finger down. Always keep the hand in the third position. $\frac{4}{0}$ = natural harmonic.

Shifting

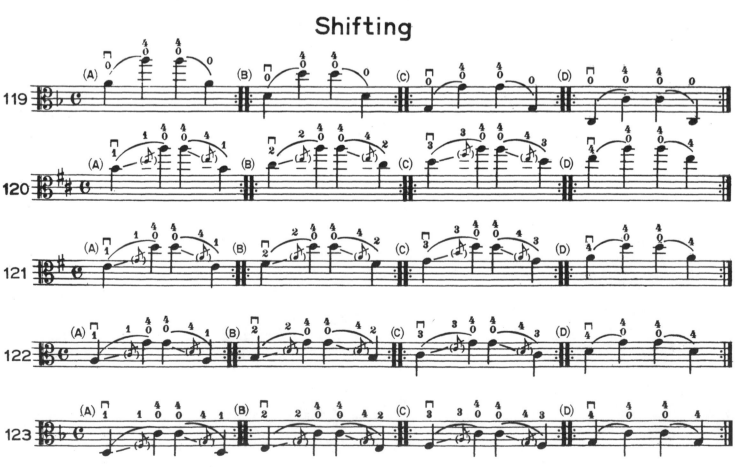

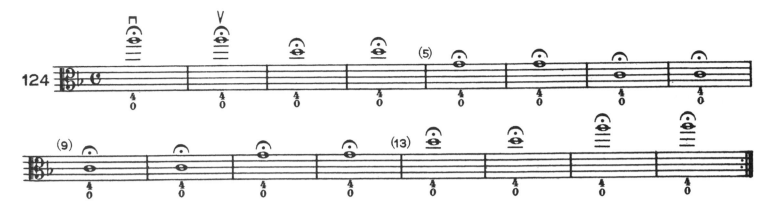

Finger Extensions

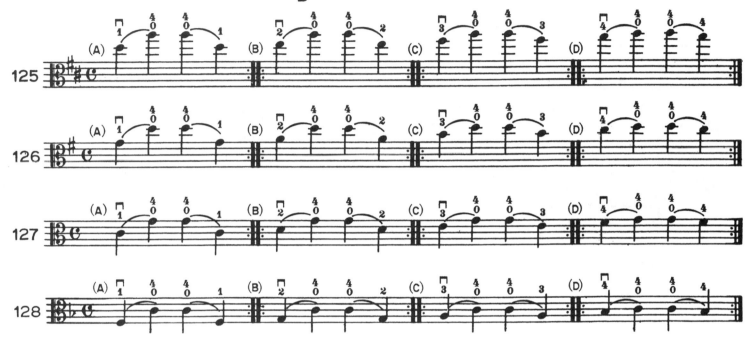

Harmonic Etude

WOHLFAHRT

Key of A Major

$\widehat{4}$ = Extend fourth finger while hand remains in same position.

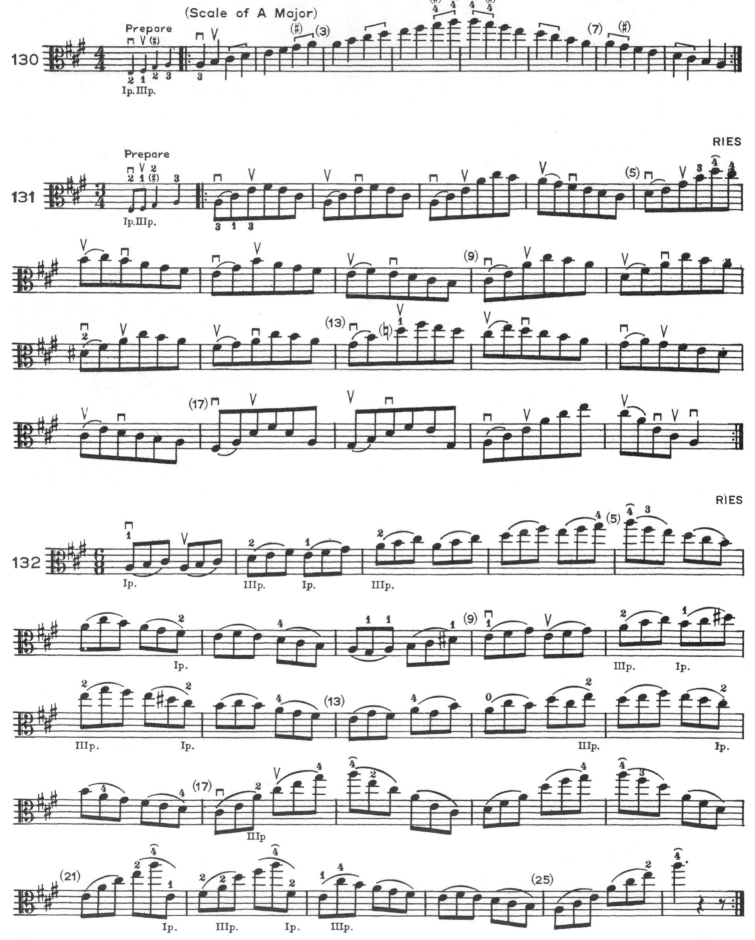

Shifting

Etude

WOHLFAHRT

25

SELECTED SOLOS IN THE FIRST AND THIRD POSITIONS

Barcarolle
from Tales of Hoffmann

OFFENBACH

Liebestraum

LISZT

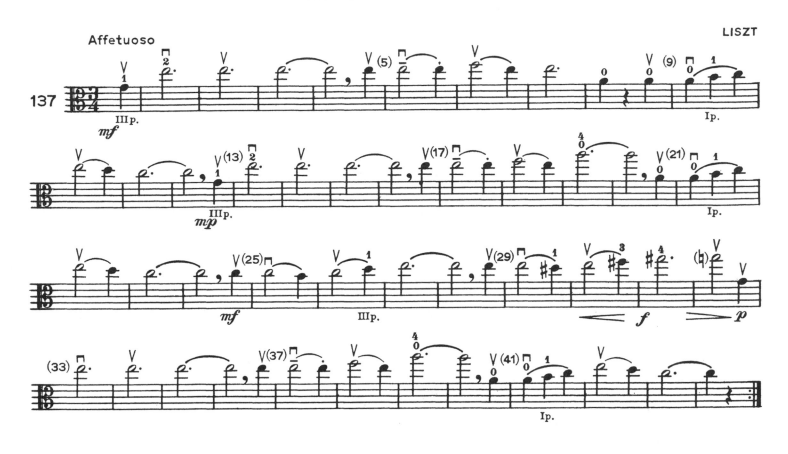

Melody

RUBINSTEIN

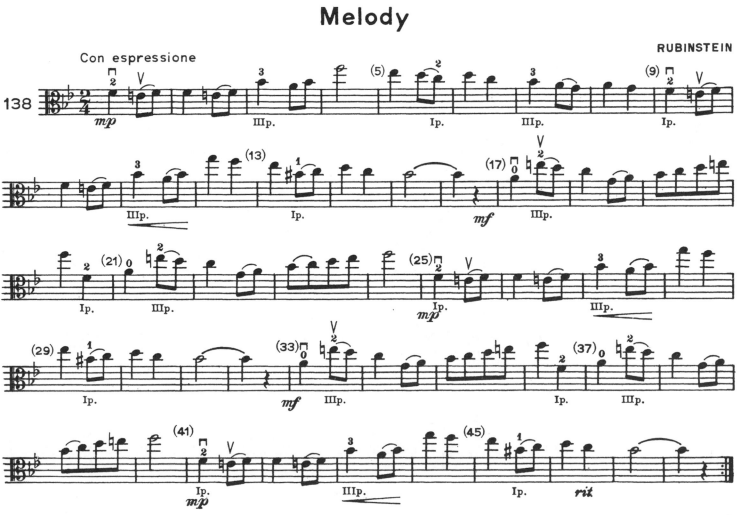

Merry Widow Waltz

FRANZ LEHAR

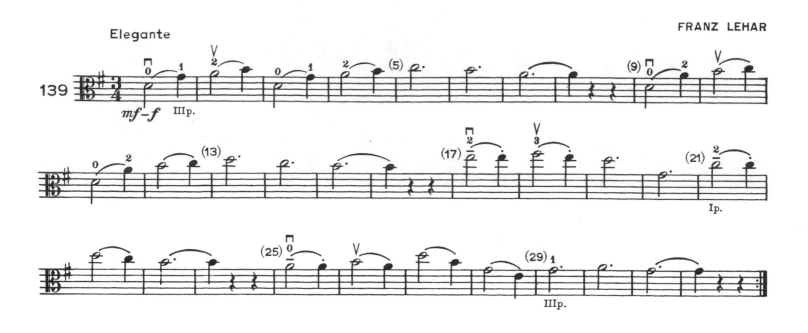

Largo
from New World Symphony

DVORAK

Nocturne

BLON

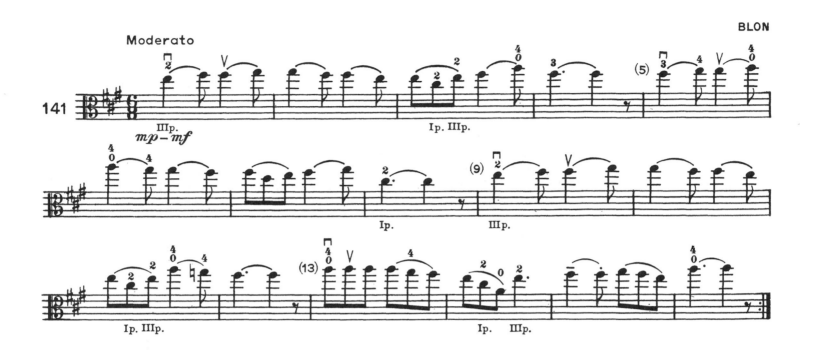

Carry Me Back to Old Virginny

JAMES A. BLAND

Theme from Fantaisie - Impromptu

CHOPIN
(Adapted)

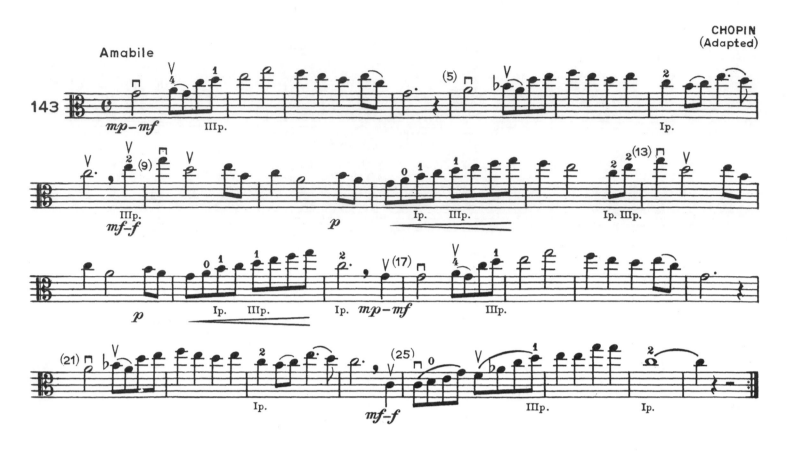

Song of the Volga Boatman

FOLK SONG

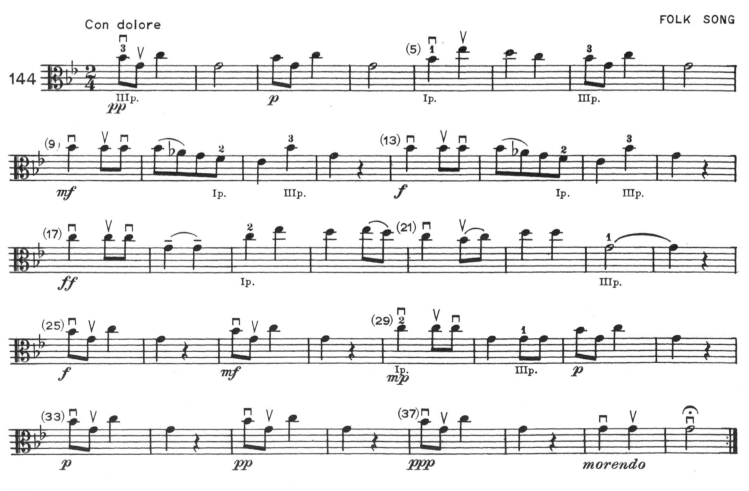

Etude Première

WOHLFAHRT

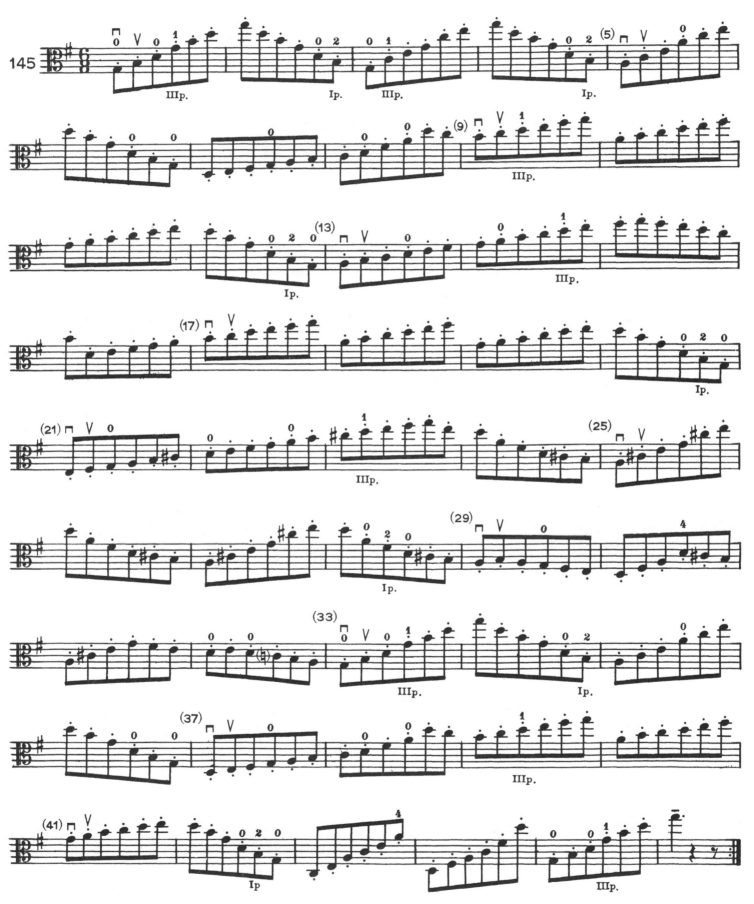

Etude de la Vélocité

CAMPAGNOLI

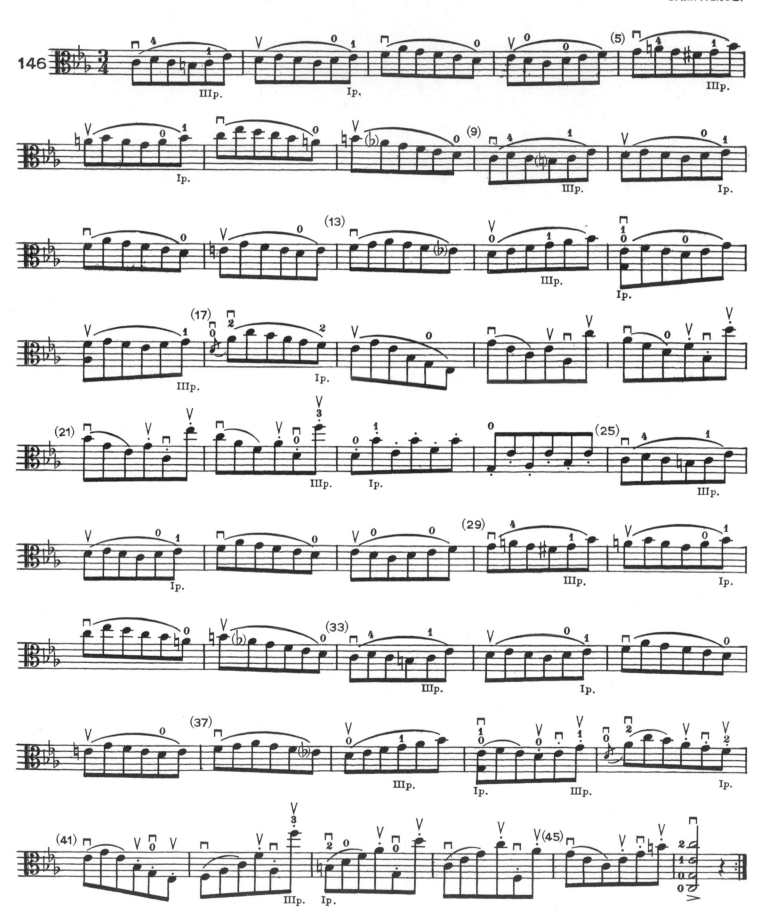

Etude Brillante

MAZAS

* Remember to extend 4th finger without changing position of hand.

Scherzo-Caprice

BLUMENSTENGEL

* Remember to extend **4th** finger without changing position of hand.

Musette
from Second Classical Suite
(DUET)

LECLAIR
Transcribed by
H. A. Hummel

*La Mélancolie
(DUET)

PRUME
Transcribed by
H. A. Hummel

Andante sentimentale

150

* The most popular duet of the 19th Century, La Mélancolie brought world-wide fame to its composer.

Capriccio Brillante
(DUET)

RODE
Transcribed by
H. A. Hummel

Theme and Variation
on the Air "Barucaba"
(DUET)

PAGANINI
Transcribed by
H. A. Hummel

The Half Position
("Saddle" or "Nut" Position)

Chromatic Fingering Chart

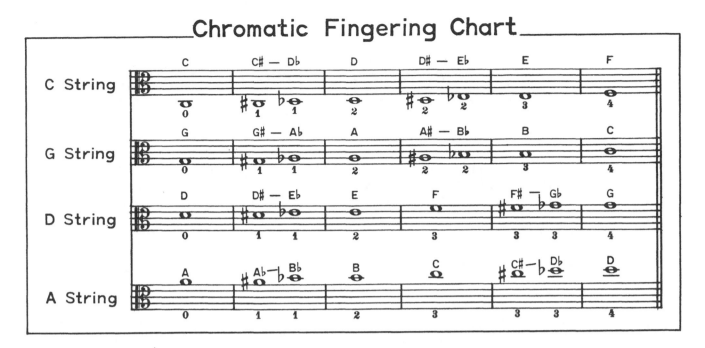

Foundation Studies in the Half Position

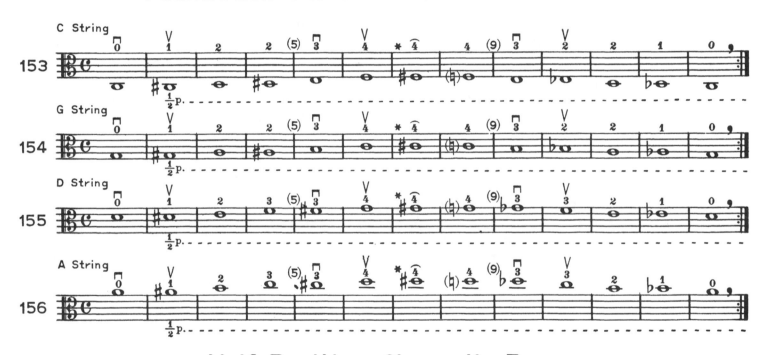

Half Position Chromatic Range

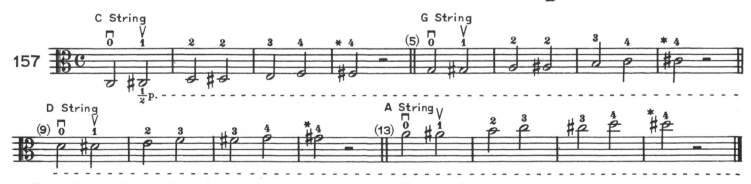

* Theoretically, the 4th finger extended is not a part of the Half Position; yet, it is necessary to use it as such in order to play chromatic progressions and melodic passages written in sharp keys.

Alternating Half and First Positions

Also practice (1) using a separate bow for each tone, and (2) slurring each two tones.

BRUNI

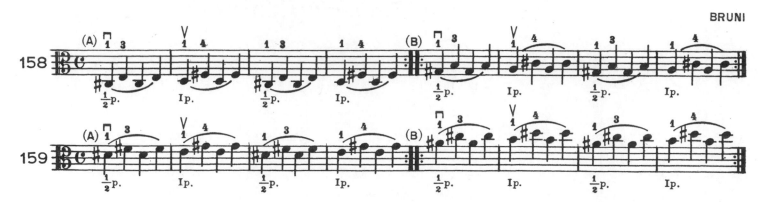

From String to String in Half Position

RITTER

Shifting from Half to First Position

CAMPAGNOLI

Technical Passages in Half and First Positions

KAYSER

DONT

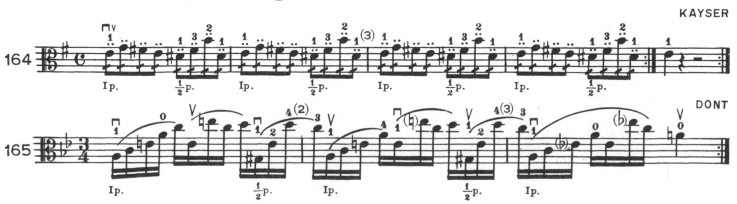

MUSICAL EXCERPTS EMPLOYING THE HALF POSITION
Scarf Dance Theme

Scarf Dance Theme — CHAMINADE

L'Abeille - Excerpt No. 1 — L. SCHUBERT

L'Abeille - Excerpt No. 2 — L. SCHUBERT

Concerto Passages — ACCOLAY (Vieuxtemps), SEITZ, RODE, VIOTTI

Half Position Etude No. 1

Also practice slowly, using a separate bow for each note.

ALARD

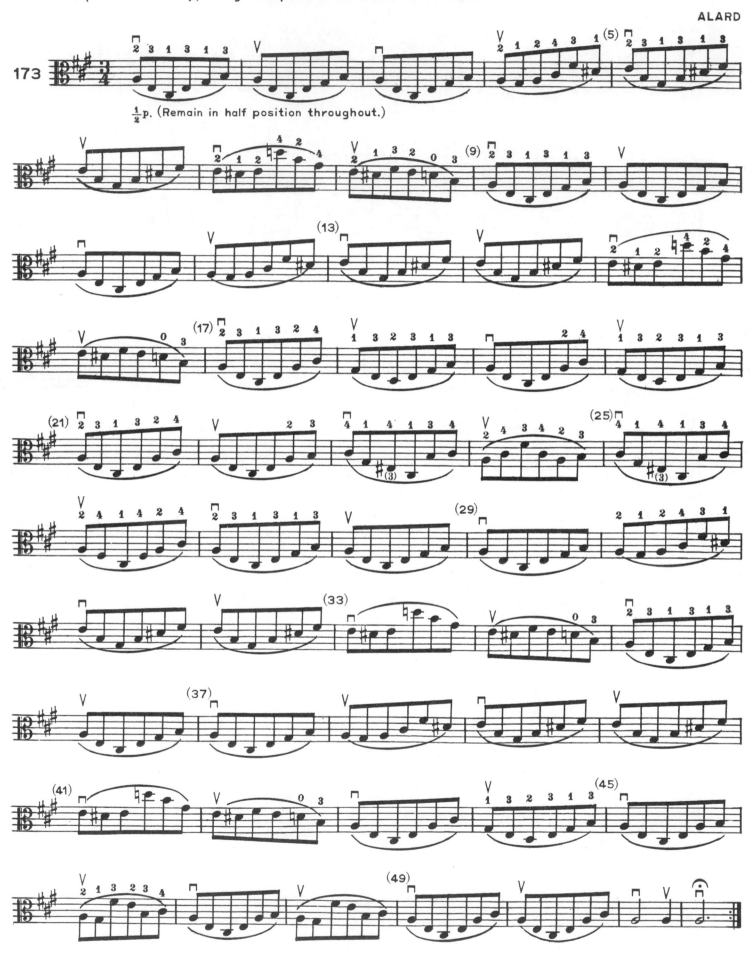

½ p. (Remain in half position throughout.)

Half Position Etude No. 2

Also practice slowly, (1) using a separate bow for each note, and (2) slurring each two notes.

BLUMENSTENGEL

Classical Caprice
(Employing Cross-Fingering and the First, Third, and Half Positions)

CORELLI

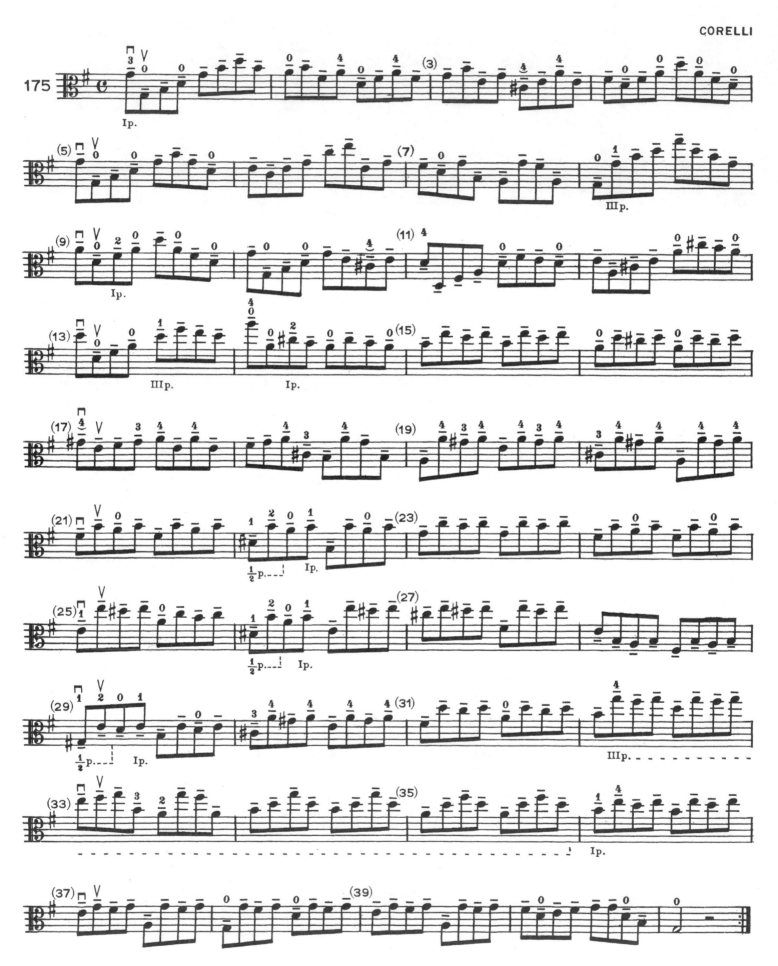

SELECTED DUETS IN THE FIRST, THIRD, AND HALF POSITIONS

Souvenir Poetique
(DUET)

DANCLA
Transcribed by
H. A. Hummel

*   2nd finger, IIIp., must touch string lightly for harmonic an octave higher than note fingered.

** 1st finger, IIIp., must touch string lightly for harmonic an octave and fifth higher than note fingered.

Concertante in D
(DUET)

CAMPAGNOLI
Transcribed by
H. A. Hummel

* $\underline{1}$ = Draw back 1st finger while hand remains in same position.

Fantaisie de Concert
(In the First, Third, and Half Positions)

SCHOEN

* Remember to draw back 1st finger without changing position of hand.